FIVE-MINUTE ★ TRUE STORIES

ANIMAL BFFs

BY AUBRE ANDRUS

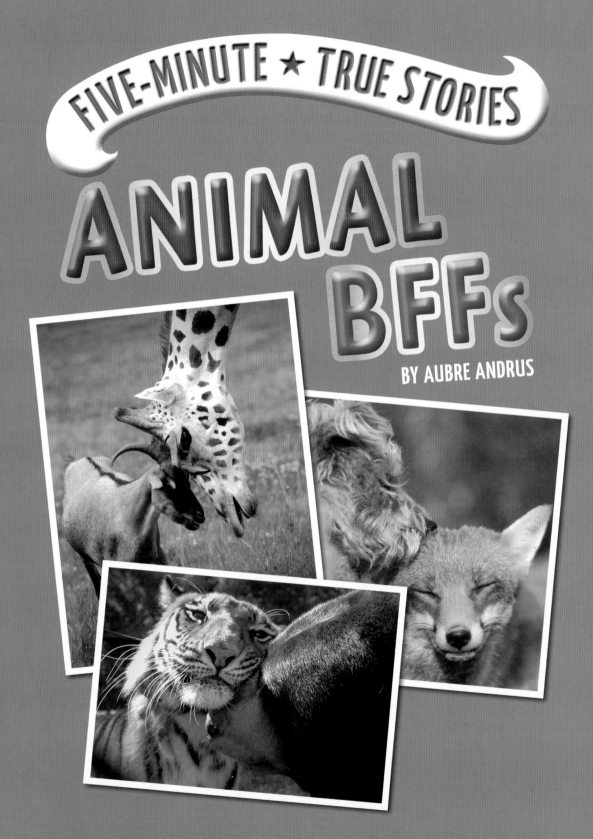

Scholastic Inc.

Library of Congress Cataloging-in-Publication Data available

ISBN 978-0-545-91419-2

10 9 8 7 6 5 4 3 2 1   16 17 18 19 20

Printed in Malaysia 108
First edition, August 2016
Book design by Jessica Meltzer

TABLE OF CONTENTS

INTRODUCTION

A tortoise and a kitten make for unlikely friends. Tortoises often live outside in the wild, and kittens love cozying up inside. Tortoises have hard shells and kittens have soft fur. Talk about opposites!

In the animal world, though, friendships come in all shapes and sizes! There is a dog that swims with dolphins, and a monkey that gets a piggyback ride from a warthog. There is even a group of buddies that includes a lion, a tiger, and a bear—oh my!

All of these amazing animal stories are true. And there's nothing better than a true friend—no matter the species!

MILO AND BONEDIGGER

Bonedigger and Milo met each other when they were just a cub and a pup, and they became fast friends. As their friendship grew, so did the two pals. But one of them grew a lot bigger than the other! Bonedigger is a 500-pound lion, and Milo is an 11-pound dachshund.

The little dog and huge cat live in the same pen together at a zoo in Oklahoma. That seems like it would be a scary sight, but Bonedigger would never hurt Milo. The animals lick each other, paw at each other, chase each other, and nibble at each other. It's all in good fun!

Lions are known as the kings of the jungle, but sometimes Bonedigger gets startled when Milo barks. Who would have thought that a pet dog could hold his own against a "fearless" wild cat? Their story might have been much different if they hadn't met each other when they were both so young.

Bonedigger was born with a disease, which made it hard for him to walk. The zookeepers decided to keep the little lion cub separate from the other animals until he was healthy. The park manager brought him home for special care. That's where Bonedigger met Milo and three other dachshund pups he now calls friends.

Because he was young and had trouble walking, the dogs weren't scared of Bonedigger. In fact, Milo and the other puppies tried to protect the lion cub even as he grew. It didn't take long before Milo and Bonedigger became best buds. They wrestled together and fought over toys just like siblings do.

As far as anyone can tell, Milo thinks Bonedigger is a really big dog—or maybe Milo considers himself a lion? The two unlikely buddies share meals of raw meat and eat side by side without fighting. Milo will even lick Bonedigger's teeth after a big meal—and those are some large teeth!

Milo sometimes tries to copy the "puffing," or loud roars, of his lion friend. While Bonedigger's roar can be heard from almost a mile away, it's unlikely that the mini sausage dog will ever be able to make a noise that loud—whether it's a bark or a roar!

Although, being loud might not be Milo's goal. Maybe he's just trying to learn the language of his lion friend. After all, it would be hard to speak a different language from your best friend.

Bonedigger is healthy now, and he and his canine pals live happily together at the zoo. It might be unusual to see dogs at a zoo, but there is no way the zookeepers can break up these friends—they're inseparable! They sleep together every night. The dachshunds like lying on top of Bonedigger like he's a giant pillow.

Whenever the dogs do separate from their lion friend, they are sure to check in with him immediately when they return. It's like Bonedigger is keeping count and making sure everyone is safe.

So while Milo was the first to protect Bonedigger, the lion is now watching over his doggie pal. That's what friends are for!

❤ ❤ ❤

GERALD AND EDDIE

Gerald the giraffe lives in a zoo in England. When he first arrived in England from Africa, he was two years old. He had a hard time making friends in his new home. He was so shy, and he was very nervous.

The zookeepers tried to introduce him to new giraffes, but he didn't get along with any of them. Everyone began to worry. Gerald must have felt lonely. The zookeepers knew he needed a friend. But who?

Eddie was born in the zoo. He's a loud, friendly goat who likes to hang out with other animals. The zookeepers decided to introduce Gerald and Eddie. Maybe Eddie could get through to Gerald and welcome him into his new home.

At first, Gerald didn't like Eddie. The two animals couldn't be more opposite. Gerald was fifteen feet tall. Eddie was a lot shorter. Gerald was shy. Eddie was confident. But soon the giraffe started to like the little goat.

When Eddie walked around, Gerald followed. Before long, the two were chasing each other around the field. Eddie made Gerald feel comfortable in his new home, and the two animals became really close. It was almost as if the giraffe thought he was a goat himself!

Gerald often leans his long giraffe neck down to nuzzle his goat friend or lick his head. After all, Eddie normally can't see eye-to-eye with the tall giraffe! Sometimes the little goat tries to jump on Gerald's neck. That's his way of cuddling his giant friend.

The two friends spend every moment together, even when they're eating. The giraffe eats from a raised platform that's closer to his eye level while the goat eats on the ground. But they still like to stand side by side during every meal. When they share a trough, which is a container for water, big Gerald lets Eddie get his nose in first.

Sometimes a zebra named Zebedee bullies Gerald. But his goat friend sticks up for him and shoos Zebedee away. Eddie is a loyal friend. The giraffe and the goat always make sure the other is happy.

The zookeepers were proud of Gerald for making a new friend, and they wanted to introduce him to a giraffe again. At first, Gerald was stubborn. He didn't want to make a new friend. He already had one!

But true to his character, Eddie stayed by Gerald's side and helped him along. When Gerald acted shy around the new giraffe, Eddie pushed him to get to know her. Gerald finally learned that the new giraffe, Genevieve, was pretty nice.

With help from Eddie, Gerald and Genevieve became good friends.

Eddie was happy because Gerald was happy. Eventually, Gerald and Genevieve went on to have two babies—one named George and one named Geoffrey. It never would have happened without help from their little friend Eddie.

Gerald and Eddie may have been opposites in both size and personality, but it doesn't mean that they couldn't be friends. If Gerald could talk, he'd say that even the smallest of friends can make the biggest difference!

❤ ❤ ❤

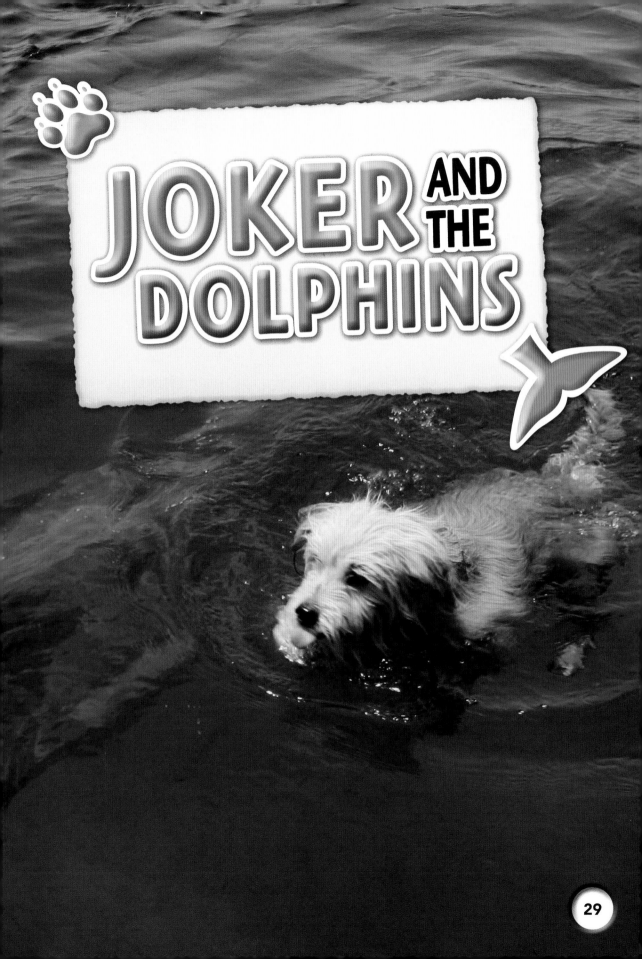

JOKER AND THE DOLPHINS

When you visit a dolphin park, you expect to see—what else? Dolphins! What you don't expect to see is a dog. But that's exactly what you'll find at this pretty beachside dolphin park in Israel.

It took some time for the friendship between Joker the dog and his dolphin family to grow. Before he befriended the dolphins, he had to charm the dolphin park staff.

The little dog first wandered into the dolphin park on his own, and the staff shooed him away. Groups of tourists had paid to swim, snorkel, and dive with dolphins, and there was no room for a stray dog at the busy park.

But the next morning, the shaggy dog trotted down the pier again. He wasn't interested in any of the people—just the dolphins. Joker had never seen anything like them! He perched at the edge of the pier to study the playful dolphins as they splashed in the sea.

Joker watched the bottlenose dolphins all day. And they watched him, too. Dolphins are naturally curious. Since he wasn't bothering any of the tourists, the staff let Joker spend the day.

When the sun set, Joker left the dolphin park. But he returned the next morning to see his dolphin friends. And the morning after that he showed up, too. The dolphin park workers couldn't believe it. Like clockwork, the dog showed up each morning to peer into the sea at the dolphins.

Then, one day, Joker was feeling brave. He leaped into the salty water. **Splash!** Joker wasn't watching anymore—he was swimming with his dolphin friends! Now the dolphin park workers had seen it all.

At first, they were worried for the little dog. What would the sea-bound creatures think of this landlocked animal now? The dolphins were surprised, but Joker was a friendly face. Soon Joker and the dolphins were swimming together every day like old friends.

Joker is a good swimmer, but he can't swim as fast as a dolphin. Bottlenose dolphins glide through the water with ease thanks to their sleek skin, body shape, and muscular tails. Joker can only dog-paddle and his fluffy fur weighs him down. But that doesn't stop him!

Eventually, Joker began to understand the dolphins. He knows when he can and can't jump in the water. When the dolphins are eating, Joker stays out of the water. When they tease him, he jumps in.

Since the dolphins and the dog were now best friends, the dolphin workers started to keep an eye on Joker. They wondered where he went every night. One worker followed him home and finally met his owner.

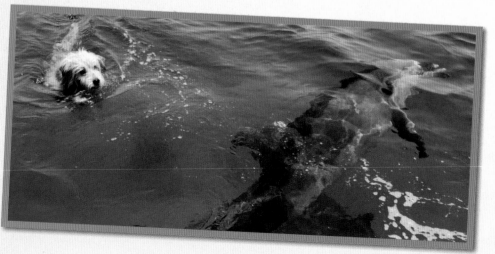

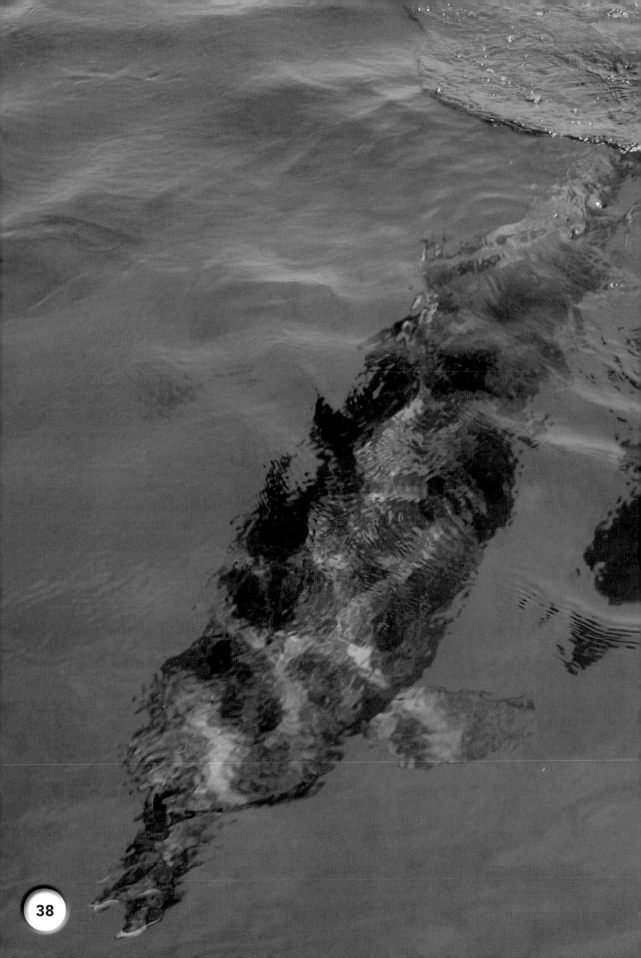

For a while, Joker would get a ride home from one of the dolphin park workers every night. But soon Joker's owner let him move in permanently at the dolphin park. Now the diving dog has become a popular sight at the dolphin park—maybe even more popular than the dolphins!

It took Joker and the dolphins a long time to form a friendship. The sleek sea creatures looked completely different from the furry pup, and they didn't understand one another's language. But getting to know one another was part of the fun of this friendship!

❤ ❤ ❤

BALOO, SHERE KHAN, AND LEO

A "BLT" is a sandwich with bacon, lettuce, and tomato. But at one zoo, "BLT" is the nickname for a bear, a lion, and a tiger. They go together even better than bacon, lettuce, and tomato!

Baloo the American black bear, Leo the African lion, and Shere Khan the Bengal tiger were just babies when they first met in Georgia. They were adopted, but their owner wasn't able to care for them properly. Someone needed to step in fast and help.

When an animal sanctuary learned about the trio of wild baby animals, they came to the rescue. An animal sanctuary is a place that cares for animals in need. The lion, the tiger, and the bear were just a few months old and the zookeepers wanted to make sure that they grew into healthy adults.

At a normal zoo, a lion, a tiger, and a bear would usually be cared for separately and would live in different areas. But Baloo, Leo, and Shere Khan got along like brothers. The keepers decided they didn't want to break up the family. They let the three growing animals live together in the same space.

In their new home, it wasn't long before the brothers began feeling better. Shere Khan the tiger cub started pouncing on Baloo and Leo and rubbing his head against their heads. Leo the lion turned out to be very calm—his favorite thing to do is nap. Baloo the bear has a big sweet tooth and was always ready for his next treat.

Although the animals were growing stronger, Baloo took a little bit longer to get healthy. He needed an operation in order to get better. The zookeepers took him away, and it was the first time the trio was apart. Shere Khan and Leo were sad.

The lion and tiger paced along the fence of their new home in Georgia. Shere Khan and Leo were worried about their missing brother. They cried out, roaring for Baloo. Once Baloo healed, he was returned to his brothers. That was the only time they'd ever been separated.

Now that they're all grown, the brothers eat together, sleep together, and play together. They can often be found cuddling, nuzzling, or licking one other. Even though they live in a large pen, they always stay near one another. They hate to be apart!

In the wild, these three friends never would have met. Not only are they different species, but they're from different parts of the world. Black bears are found in North America, lions are found in Africa, and tigers are found in Asia—those are three different continents. It's not like these animals could just hop on a plane to visit one another!

But somehow a 400-pound tiger, a 500-pound lion, and a 700-pound bear have become best friends. People who visit the zoo think the trio teaches a great lesson about friendship. It doesn't matter what you look like or where you come from, you can still be friends—or even family!

❤ ❤ ❤

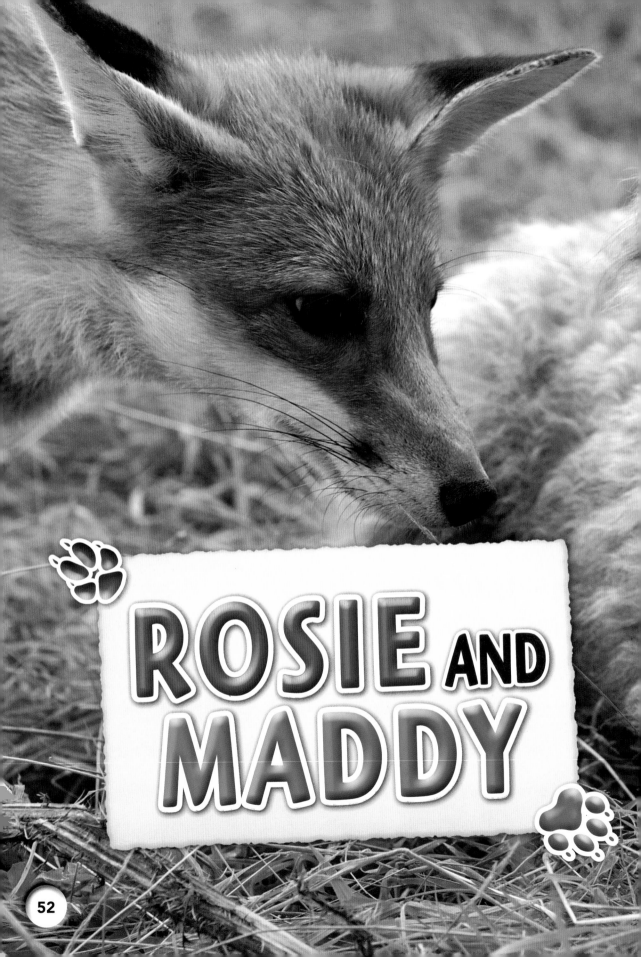

ROSIE AND MADDY

Fox cubs, or kits, are born with their eyes closed. Rosie was just a little fox cub when she was found alone in the woods in Great Britain. Her eyes weren't open, which meant she was only a few weeks old. Her mom and dad couldn't be found anywhere.

Luckily, a family adopted the little fox cub and took her home. Rosie didn't know it, but there was even more luck in store for her. When Rosie arrived at her new home, a furry dog named Maddy was there to greet her. Maddy began to lick the young fox like she was a puppy. The friendly dog would soon become her new best friend.

Having a fox for a pet is a bit unusual. The family wanted to house-train Rosie so she could live inside. They looked to Maddy for help. She had always been a gentle dog and helped her owners care for injured wildlife before.

Maddy took the job seriously. She showed the fox cub what it was like to live in a home. The fox cub learned quickly. Before long, Rosie learned how to sit. Then she learned how to earn a treat. Finally, she learned how to go outside when she needed to use the bathroom. Rosie is very smart! And Maddy was a good teacher. The fox cub looked up to the terrier, and soon they became great friends.

Rosie started acting like a pet dog and even perched on top of the couch like her furry friend does. Dogs and foxes have a lot in common. They're both active and like to play. So after learning tricks, it was time for some fun.

The two pals love to jump on top of each other and roll in the grass. Rosie is smaller and loves to dive onto Maddy and surprise her. They chase each other around the vegetable patch in their backyard and sometimes in the house. When they play inside, they act just as crazy, which makes the house a mess!

Once Rosie grew bigger, she had to be moved outside to the backyard. Maddy visits her every day and greets her with a wagging tail. They love chasing sticks that their owner throws for them.

The furry friends sometimes fight like sisters. Whenever Maddy has something, Rosie wants it. She wants to be just like her big sis. If the dog has a stick in her mouth, then the little fox is going to jump all over her to try to get it!

When Rosie doesn't get what she wants, she makes noises. Foxes can make all kinds of sounds. Maddy doesn't know what they mean exactly, but she probably understands that the little fox is mad. It's easy to understand a fit!

At the end of the day, the two friends love to cuddle with each other. Sometimes, Rosie jumps into Maddy's bed to snuggle with her even though the bed is only meant for one dog.

Maddy is a mixed terrier, the same kind of breed that hunts foxes for sport in England. Other dogs like her may have seen a fox and thought it was an enemy. But when Maddy met Rosie, all she saw was a friend.

Everyone deserves a chance. You never know where you'll find your next BFF!

❤ ❤ ❤

MIWA-CHAN AND URIBO

Piggyback rides are fun, even in the animal kingdom. Baby monkeys love to ride on their mothers' backs. They feel extra safe when they're near their mothers, and they can get around more quickly. But what happens when a baby's mother is not there? One baby monkey hitched a ride from an unexpected driver in Japan!

It all started when zookeepers introduced Miwa-chan, a Japanese monkey, to Uribo, a wild piglet. At first, the piglet wasn't sure what to do with his new monkey friend. That is, until Miwa-chan jumped on his back!

The zookeepers couldn't believe it. Miwa-chan was getting a piggyback ride on the back of a pig! The piggyback ride probably helped Miwa-chan feel safe, just like he would have felt if he were riding on his mother's back.

You see, Miwa-chan had been found in the wild, alone and scared. The little baby didn't have a mother to protect him. Because he didn't have a family, the zoo adopted him.

Miwa-chan was safe in the zoo, but he was sad. He cried out at night. The zookeepers knew he was lonely. After all, monkeys usually have large families, and Miwa-chan probably missed his mom. They decided he needed a friend to keep him company.

Uribo already lived at the zoo. Even though a pig and a monkey are totally different creatures, they had a lot in common. The piglet was also found alone in the wild, just like Miwa-chan. So Uribo was lonely, too.

The zookeepers thought the two orphans might be the perfect fit for each other, and they were right! Miwa-chan and Uribo have so much fun together that they now live in the same home at the zoo.

The two friends love going for walks together—usually with Miwa-chan on the back of his pig pal. Even as the little monkey grows older, he still likes hopping on Uribo for a ride. Uribo doesn't mind. Maybe he knows it makes the monkey feel safe.

In order to stay on Uribo's back, Miwa-chan has to be really good at balancing. Especially when Uribo runs around. It's a good thing that monkeys' feet are almost the same as their hands—they can grip tightly with either. That's why monkeys are so good at swinging from branches high in the trees. They can hold on to a tree or to the fur on a wild pig's back.

A pig with fur? That's right! Wild pigs are different from their barnyard cousins. They have scruffy brown fur instead of smooth pink skin. Also, wild pigs have straight tails while pigs on a farm have curly tails.

The two friends might look different, but they can always be found side by side. And now they've become famous in Japan! Visitors love to watch them play together and go for rides. Millions of people who can't see their friendship in person have watched videos online of the unlikely pair.

People love that Uribo comforted Miwa-chan even though he needed comforting, too. It's amazing that one little act of kindness between two friends could become so big!

❤ ❤ ❤

Mickey loves her dog, Osiris. They live in an apartment in Chicago, where Osiris has a lot of dog friends. He likes to look out the window and watch people—and dogs!—walk around the city streets.

On Valentine's Day, Mickey visited a pet store in the city and saw a cute baby rat. He was so little and his eyes were barely open. Mickey fell in love! She decided to take him home. She named him Riff Ratt.

Mickey is trained to care for wild animals, and she acts as a foster mother to many pets that need homes. That means she brings a pet into her house and cares for it until someone is ready to adopt it. So Osiris has met, played with, and helped care for many furry friends including newborn kittens, puppies, and even baby squirrels!

But Osiris had never seen a rat before. Mickey wondered what he would think of a little rodent. Luckily, he was ready to take on Riff Ratt as his next patient. Riff Ratt was so tiny that Mickey had to feed him milk with a syringe. Osiris sat by her side and licked up any spilled milk.

Soon, Riff Ratt got bigger and stronger. When he finally opened his eyes, he saw his family—and he knew the dog was a part of it. Rats are cautious creatures, so at first, Riff Ratt liked hiding in Mickey's shirt pocket because he felt cozy and safe.

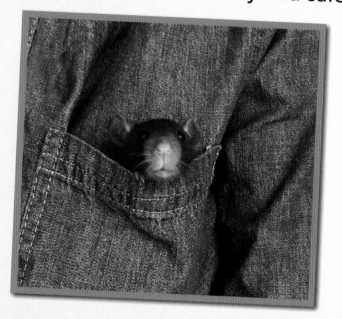

But rats are also curious. They love to explore! So do dogs. It wasn't long before the tiny rat and the big dog became fast friends, and they started wandering around the apartment side by side.

Osiris always plays gently with Riff Ratt. Sometimes he'll even pet his rat friend lightly with the pad of his paw. Mickey calls them a "dynamic duo" because they spend all of their time together. If one can't find the other, they get worried.

The two friends play together and love to share toys. When Osiris plays with a toy, like a tennis ball, Riff Ratt wants in on the fun. They like to chew the fuzz off tennis balls together—Riff Ratt gets on one side and Osiris gets on the other. Even though the toys are meant for a dog and are sometimes larger than Riff Ratt, he doesn't mind!

Sometimes Osiris acts a bit like a rat. Riff Ratt loves to eat vegetables so now Osiris does, too! But they do more than just eat together—Riff Ratt likes to crawl into the big dog's mouth! It looks pretty scary when you see a tail hanging out of a dog's mouth. But Osiris doesn't bite. His knows his rat pal is just trying to lick his teeth.

The big dog's tongue is almost the same size as Riff Ratt. So when Osiris licks Riff Ratt, he almost knocks the little guy over! Riff Ratt knows it's a sign of love. The small rodent's tongue is so tiny, but that doesn't stop him from giving Osiris "kisses," too. He licks Osiris's nose all the time. He'll even lick inside his nostrils. Yuck! But Osiris just sits patiently and waits for his friend to finish.

When they cuddle together, Riff Ratt lays next to Osiris's cheek. He's much smaller than his dog pal, but the little rat might not realize just how tiny he is. He often stands on his two hind legs. That might be his way of feeling taller next to his dog friend.

It's not always easy for two different animals to be such good friends. Osiris knows the little rat isn't the same as his other dog pals. But he likes that Riff Ratt is different. It keeps their friendship interesting!

❤ ❤ ❤

BAMBI AND BEN

The Disney movie *Bambi* begins when Bambi loses his mother. Luckily, his woodland forest friends, like Thumper the rabbit, cheer him up and become his family. This story is the same—but it's true!

During a bad storm one night in Montana, a baby deer sat shivering, cold, and wet on the side of a dark road. He was alone. His mom had accidentally been hit by a car, and now he was an orphan. He didn't know what to do.

A driver saw the little fawn and pulled over. She didn't want to leave him there. It was hard for drivers to see during the storm, and more cars were headed that way. The fawn was unhurt, but he was so scared. The driver wrapped him in her jacket. Then she picked up the baby deer and placed him in her car. She decided to call him Bambi.

Bambi was still scared when he got to his new home. But there were other animals inside to greet him. First he met a German shepherd named Stasha. Bambi didn't want to drink the milk that his new family tried to feed him, but Stasha made him try it so he'd feel better. They were right. He needed to eat!

Stasha the dog stayed with Bambi the next few days and comforted him. One week later, Bambi was feeling great, and the storms had passed. He ventured outside to explore his new home. Outside, there were even more furry friends! The big yard was near a barn and lots of wild animals.

The first animals Bambi met were a group of rabbits. They sniffed one another and touched noses. Then they started to play. The rabbits hopped around the yard and Bambi followed their furry tails—he even pulled on them with his teeth. Ouch! But he was just playing.

Bambi and one rabbit, named Ben, became really good friends. Rabbits like to eat dandelions, so Bambi thought he'd give the yellow flowers a try like his pal. But the rabbits thought, "Hey, that's our lunch!" and pulled the flowers from Bambi's mouth. When they were done eating, they headed to the barn to cuddle together and rest.

Bambi played with the rabbits in the barn every day. He even got to play with more dogs—and cats, too. The dogs liked to play tag with him. The cats liked to lick him. Bambi had found a great new family!

One afternoon, a few deer wandered into the yard. They noticed Bambi and wanted to get to know him. Bambi was shy at first. He didn't want to leave his old friends. Then he gathered some courage and began to play with the new deer friends. He was glad he did because it was fun!

The deer kept coming back to visit Bambi. Soon, he was playing more and more with his deer friends and less and less with his rabbit, dog, and cat friends. Finally, he decided it was time for him to live with the other deer.

It was sad when Bambi left. The animals all missed him. But one day, Bambi came back to visit! It was such a surprise, and his old pals, especially Ben, were so happy.

Bambi realized that it's okay to make new friends as long as you remember to keep the old ones, too. One can never have too many friends—human or furry!

❤ ❤ ❤

SUNSHADE
AND THE
GUINEA PIGS

Can a pet have a pet? That's the question Elaine asked herself after she noticed some unusual behavior from her dog.

Elaine often took her Airedale terrier, Sunshade, to the pet store. Every time, Sunshade ran straight to the guinea pig aisle. She'd stare for hours with her nose pressed against the glass, watching the little guinea pigs play. She looked like she wanted to join in on the fun.

Elaine knew Sunshade loved the guinea pigs, but it seemed silly to buy a pet for a pet! Still, every time they went to the pet store, Sunshade would run to the guinea pig aisle and Elaine would eventually have to pull her away.

Five years later, Sunshade got really sick. Elaine knew there was only one way to cheer her up: with a pet guinea pig. Today was the day that her pet was getting a pet. Elaine brought home a brown female guinea pig named Meatball. Sunshade was overjoyed. Her dreams had finally come true!

The dog and the guinea pig became fast friends. Sunshade snuggled gently with her much smaller buddy. Sometimes Meatball slept on top of Sunshade, and other times they cuddled next to each other for hours on the dog bed.

Elaine knew that guinea pigs don't like to live alone—even when they have a dog as a best friend. So Elaine brought home another friend for Meatball, a black female guinea pig named Sesame. Now there were two guinea pigs for Sunshade! The three friends got along great.

Sunshade was very protective of her guinea pig buddies. She liked to keep her "piggies" close to her. Sunshade was extra-nervous when Elaine's other pets were nearby, like a fat rabbit named Juice and another Airedale terrier named Jaffa.

On Christmas Eve, something unexpected happened when Elaine went to visit the guinea pigs in their cage. She didn't find two guinea pigs in the cage—she found five! It turns out that Sesame was actually a boy guinea pig, and Meatball had three babies overnight! Sunshade couldn't have been happier. The babies were all girls. Elaine named them Squeaky, Dumpling, and Ketchup.

Sunshade became the "piggy nanny," and she cared for Squeaky, Dumpling, and Ketchup as if they were her own puppies. She licked them dry after baths. She cuddled with them afterward to keep them warm.

She even shared treats with them—raw carrots! When Elaine set up a cage outside for the guinea pigs to play in, Sunshade sat by its side and guarded her friends.

Sunshade and her "piggies" were more than friends—they were a big happy family. And families are there for one another in good times and in bad times.

Elaine decided that Sunshade was not just an Airedale terrier. She was a *Superdale*. Sunshade the Superdale and her "piggies" proved that family is bigger than just the people you are related to. And when you share your love, you'll be loved in return.

❤ ❤ ❤

KASI AND MTANI

Dogs and cats aren't supposed to get along. Especially when they are a pet dog and a wild cheetah! But that's exactly what happened at one zoo in Florida.

After Kasi the cheetah cub was born, his mother couldn't care for him. Zookeepers had to step in when he was just a few weeks old. Luckily, they were able to nurse tiny Kasi into a strong, healthy cub.

The zookeepers knew that male cheetahs are very social and that Kasi would want someone his age to play with. There wasn't another litter of cheetah cubs nearby, so the zookeepers decided to introduce him to a different kind of furry friend: a dog.

Kasi was eight weeks old when he was introduced to another rescued animal, a Labrador retriever puppy. The fluffy cheetah cub was still much smaller than the playful puppy, but they got along great. The puppy was named Mtani, which means "close friend" in the African language Swahili.

In the beginning, the fast friends had a hard time understanding each other's languages. When they are young, puppies like to interact with their surroundings by using their mouths. Kittens like to use their feet. But after a few months, Mtani and Kasi understood each other just fine and spent every moment together.

During the day, Kasi and Mtani chased each other—sometimes right into a waterfall! They jumped playfully on top of each other. They pawed at each other and stole toys from each other. They napped together, cuddled together, and even groomed each other.

As the two friends grew, their fame grew, too. Visitors loved to watch the dog and cheetah pals goof off together at the zoo. The zookeepers took Mtani and Kasi on TV shows in New York and California, and to visit schools. Everybody loved the furry twosome.

On Kasi's first birthday, Mtani, the zookeepers, and visitors helped him celebrate with a special "meat cake." The two friends were growing quickly. Although cheetahs are the fastest land animal, Mtani could keep up with Kasi when they were both young. But eventually the cheetah cub outgrew his puppy pal. The two friends would outgrow each other in another way, too.

As he grew older, Kasi became curious about the other cheetahs at the zoo. He had never spent time with them before. The zookeepers noticed his interest, so they introduced him to a kind cheetah named Jenna. Jenna didn't like Kasi at first. He didn't act like a normal cheetah—he acted like a dog!

But soon Jenna taught Kasi how to behave like a cheetah. Months later, he was hanging out with his cheetah friends more than his canine companion, Mtani.

But Mtani made some new friends, too. She was happy hanging out with the zookeepers and other humans like a normal dog. And once Kasi began living with his cheetah friends, the zookeepers found Mtani a new home, too. She got to move out of the zoo and into a home with a new family—and a pet cat! Good thing Mtani isn't afraid of feline friends!

Even though Mtani and Kasi have grown apart, they had something very special during their time together at the zoo. Sometimes friendships don't last forever, but the memories always will.

❤ ❤ ❤

MORRIS AND CHAMPY

Morris loves to go horseback riding. Every morning, he hops on his chestnut-brown horse, Champy, for a sunrise trot. But there's one thing that's unusual about this story—Morris is a cat!

Jennifer lives in Australia with her pet horse, Champy, and her black cat, Morris. When she brought Morris home from the animal shelter, she never imagined that he would become her horse's best friend.

It all started when Morris began lounging lazily on the front porch. Champy took notice of the furry feline. But Morris wasn't interested in the attention. He had never met a horse before, and horses are a lot bigger than cats. That could be scary for a small cat like Morris.

But Champy was persistent. He wanted to be friends with Jennifer's new pet. Champy began grooming Morris. When horses show affection, they lick, nuzzle, and lean into one another. So that's what Champy did to Morris. The cat was puzzled, but he didn't run away. He realized pretty quickly that Champy was just acting friendly.

One day, Morris jumped on Champy's back. Jennifer couldn't believe it! It seemed like Morris wanted to show Champy that he was ready to be friends. He started grooming the big horse's mane and tail with his tongue. That's a big job for a tiny cat!

Once the two felt comfortable with each other, Champy started walking around while Morris was sitting on his back. As long as Champy is wearing a special rug or saddle pad on his back, Morris feels safe and isn't scared of slipping off.

Morris goes on rides with Champy basically every day. The cold, wind, and rain don't stop him from visiting his best friend. Whenever Morris feels like a ride, he climbs onto a fence post. Champy knows that means it's time for a trot. It's like a bus pulling up to a bus stop!

Once Champy trots over, Morris hops on his back from the fence post. Then Champy takes him wherever he'd like to go. Sometimes he'll give Morris a ride before he's even eaten his breakfast! When the horse wants to pause and graze for a bit, Morris stays on his back and lets his friend take a break.

Morris goes for horseback rides so often that Jennifer has to compete with the kitty for riding time! Jennifer needs to train Champy, but it's hard to pull Morris away from his best friend. So while Jennifer is working with Champy, Morris will watch his friend from the sidelines.

Jennifer bought Morris a special horse-riding jacket to wear in the cold weather. After all, Morris spends more time horseback riding than Jennifer does!

Champy is an incredibly friendly horse. He's tried to befriend Jennifer's other cat, Winston, again and again, but Winston is too shy. And the friendliness doesn't stop there. Since they live in Australia, kangaroos and baby joeys will sometimes bounce by the fences. Champy tries to make friends with them, too!

Champy knows you can never have too many friends, and you can never run out of kindness. After all, a small act of kindness can lead to big things—like a great friend!

❤ ❤ ❤

TARRA AND BELLA

An elephant sanctuary isn't a typical place for a dog to call home. But when a stray dog named Bella wandered into this safe space, she found more than just a home—she found a best friend, too.

Tarra the elephant used to be a star. She performed in circuses and zoos all across the country. After years of working, it was time for Tarra to retire and rest. She headed to The Elephant Sanctuary in Tennessee, a place that cares for elephants. Many elephants live there happily and are allowed to roam free. Tarra knew she would fit in perfectly.

When Tarra arrived, she was lonely and didn't know anyone. Often, a new elephant quickly becomes best friends with another elephant at the sanctuary. Tarra hadn't found an "ele-friend" yet. But she was interested in someone else: a furry white dog named Bella.

Bella was not the first stray dog to wander into The Elephant Sanctuary. There are about a dozen dogs wandering around the area. Usually, the dogs and elephants ignore one another. But that wasn't the case for Bella and Tarra. They became instant friends.

The owners of The Elephant Sanctuary couldn't believe it! How could a dog and an elephant become friends? On the outside, these two animals were nothing alike. Bella had soft fur while Tarra had tough skin. Tarra weighed 8,700 pounds, and Bella was more than 100 times smaller.

But elephants and dogs have more in common than you think. They are both social creatures, which means they like to have a friend by their side. They're also both smart, loyal, and have better memories than most other animals.

Bella and Tarra not only became great friends—they became inseparable. They ate together, drank together, slept together, and played together. They loved to run around the sanctuary, swim in ponds, and take cuddle breaks under the warm sun. They even played in the snow together! The two BFFs were always spotted side-by-side.

One day, Bella hurt her back. She couldn't walk or wag her tail. The caretakers at the sanctuary brought Bella inside their office to nurse her back to health. Tarra didn't know what was going on, just that her friend was missing. She was terribly sad without her companion.

So the big elephant stayed right outside Bella's door. Instead of roaming the sanctuary, Tarra waited. And waited some more. Everyone noticed how much the friends missed each other.

The caretakers knew they had to do something. So after a few days, they carried Bella outside to the balcony so she could see her elephant pal standing guard below. Bella's tail started wagging! The friends were so happy to see each other, even though it was only for a little bit. Every day after that, Bella was allowed to visit with Tarra outside.

Slowly, Bella started to feel better, especially with daily visits from her "ele-friend." Three weeks later, Bella was released. Tarra petted her best bud with her trunk and made loud noises to show how excited she was. The little dog would even roll onto her back and let Tarra stroke her stomach with her foot.

Tarra and Bella were gentle, patient, and trusting. They were kind and protective of each other. Their friendship may seem unusual, but it's no different than the friendship between you and your best friend. Something that looks different on the outside could be perfectly normal on the inside. Bella and Tarra prove that!

❤ ❤ ❤

PHOTO CREDITS